Author: David Lee Webb Sr.

I0414974

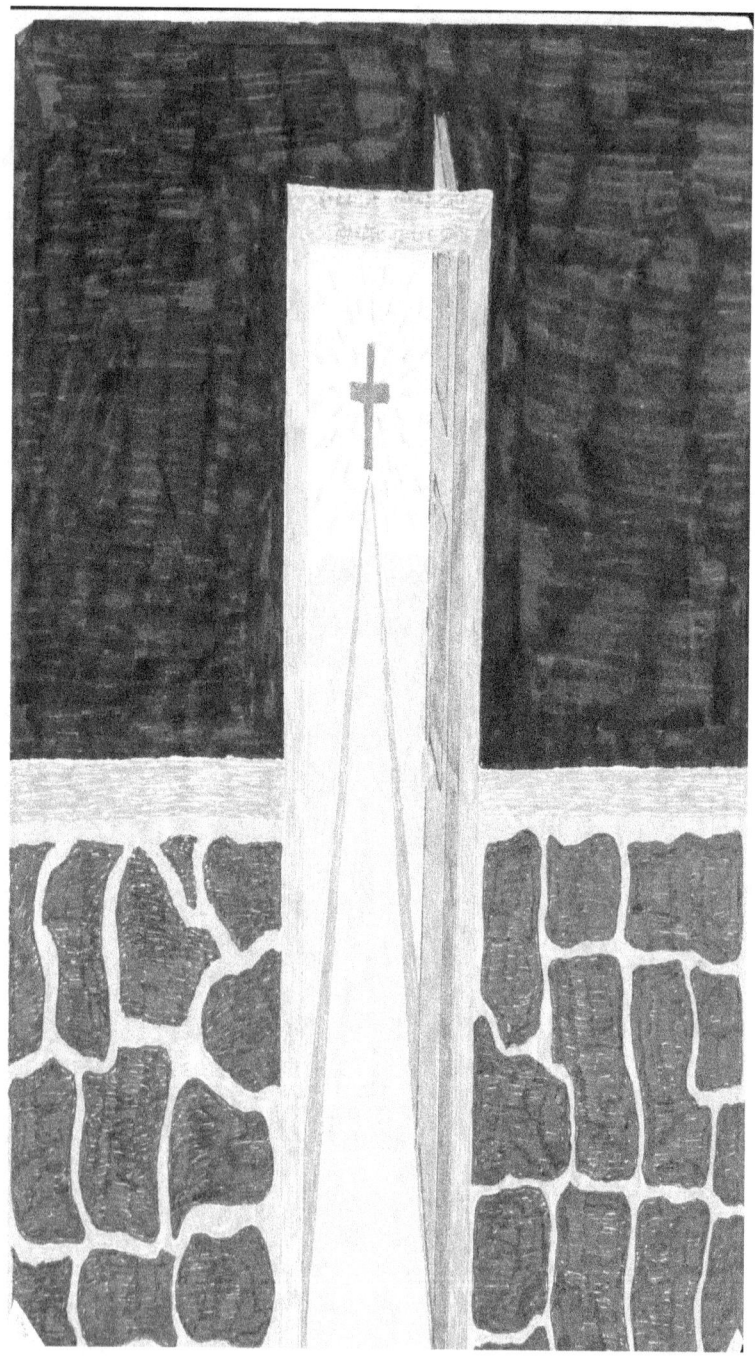

This book is dedicated to all those who struggle in life to come to terms with the truth about life…

To those who suffer from addiction and alcoholism, to the **Chaplains, Counselors,** and **Pastors** who help those who are afflicted. To our **Veterans** and our **Disabled Veterans** along with their families.

To my Wife Gloria and our children Charlie, Kasandra, David Jr. and Nathaniel

Romans 10:9

That if thou shalt confess with thy mouth the Lord JESUS, and shalt believe in thine heart that GOD hath raised him from the dead, thou shalt be saved.

About this Book

This book is written from the heart. It contains a variety of ways to approach a new way of life for the troubling times we live in. The times have become very evil. Seeing the impacts of the deceptions that occur in business, our societies, the internet, loss of family values, corrupt governments and all the people keep supporting such wrong doings. Since we keep following the ways of man,

man hasn't solved any issues of hunger, becoming debt free, creating more jobs, uncontrolled debt, nor have they turned to **GOD through JESUS CHRIST**. We are witnessing our end times of what used to be a great country at one point. Look at what man did to the Indian tribes… These are but a few of the issues that have brought this country to its knees and we are only a step away from being taken captive and controlled by another country. Judgment is coming, what choice will you make? To follow the folly of man and his ways? Or to set your own heart and house in order and amend your ways through **CHRIST JESUS with GOD?**

These things that I have written about, I have let them lead me down many a wrong path...I was blind to such corrupt ways and oblivious to the impact and draining of one's life. These are the

ways of the world, that don't
follow **GOD'S WAYS**

TABLE OF CONTENTS

Chapter   1

As humans, we have not the capacity to fathom how great GOD really is. We can however, come to a partial understanding.

1 Corinthians 13:9

For we know in part, and we prophesy in part.

So for many, if not all of us, have been taught with

incomplete instruction. Chances are we have been taught about the wrath bearing GOD with fire and brimstone. That is nothing but a half-truth! They that taught in this manner, may have not mentioned that GOD is a GOD of LOVE, A GOD of PEACE, A GOD of MERCY who wants us to awaken to his ways and to mature .

For our immature ways along with our twisted misconceptions of our self-will and our actions have greatly hindered many a blessing from above. We have simply and most arrogantly denied GOD and HIS WAYS... and for what? Money?, Pleasures?, Haughtiness?, Lusts of the world?, Drugs?, Alcohol?, Self-seeking of all our false so-called feel good now stuff of the world? Shame on us for not humbling ourselves and truly learning for ourselves who GOD truly is! We rely on others,

when in fact the responsibility is ours to research.

Study to show thyself approved unto GOD, a workman that needeth not to be ashamed, rightly dividing the word of truth.

Our current time is stated in

2 Timothy 3:1-7

1) *This know also, that in the last days perilous times shall come.*

2) *For men shall be lovers of their own selves, covetous, boasters, proud, blasphemers, disobedient to parents, unthankful, unholy,*

3) *Without natural affection, trucebreakers, false accusers, incontinent, (without self-control), fierce, despisers of those that are good.*

4) *Traitors, heady, highminded, lovers of*

pleasures more than lovers of GOD;

5) *Having a form of GODLINESS, but denying the power there of: from such turn away.*

6) *For of sort are they which creep into houses, and lead captive silly women laden with sins, led away with diverse lusts,*

7) *Ever learning, and never able to come to the truth.*

I don't want to seem so callous, however, I had to get the point across how we have made the wrong decisions because we have been asleep at the wheel, or one other way it can be put is... It lets us know there is a problem.

How can we fix it? Our perception is a good place to start. We stop the swearing, we choose to be honest and truthful, we need willingness, and we need to have an open-mind. Next is a really big step, we pray the following prayer and accept our humility:

LORD JESUS, I know I am a sinner and I have lived my life by the ways of the world, I ask you for your forgiveness and I am asking you to come into my heart to be with me and guide me and show me a new life. I know that you laid your life down on the cross for us so that we may have everlasting life with you by the shedding of your blood for us.

In JESUS CHRIST'S name I pray. Amen

1) You need JESUS in your life.
2) We need courage, hope, and faith.
3) And we need to believe! Why do I say this? Because this worked for me, but

don't just take my word for it. Go and look up the verses that I give to you in the next chapter and see for yourself. If you are serious about sobriety and want to do it right.

4) Then you will follow what I am telling you about. Pull out all your reservations and doubt and get rid of the procrastination. For the doubt and procrastination have

done nothing more than keep you on a path of destruction.

5) Unload your fear and ask for some faith from GOD.

6) I tell you it is a beautiful journey, and if you are sincere, it beats the daylights out of what the world has to offer.

Chapter 2

Who is JESUS? Who is GOD?

You see, JESUS is the Son of GOD. In these next verses, I will do my best to show you the facts from scripture. Here is your first test of changing your perception. If you have doubts, remove them just for the moment and open your mind and your heart. You need to understand that GOD will never let his word be compromised, regardless of what false claims man makes. Let's make one thing clear; man has not any power over GOD'S WORD. If you read GOD'S WORD with a pure heart, the truth will be there. Man has only ignorance and deception and a failure to admit that they honestly don't know an answer and have too much pride for fear of being honest or truthful. Now with that said, we can get to the verses.

John 4:24

GOD is a spirit; and they that worship him must worship him in spirit and truth.

I underlined "GOD is a spirit" because this is a very important point.

Going to chapter 1 of the book of John;

John 1:1

In the beginning was the Word, and the Word was with GOD, and the word was GOD.

John 1:2

The same was in the beginning with GOD.

Did you see the implication of the word?

1) **Not only was the <u>Word with GOD</u>;**
2) **<u>The Word was GOD.</u>**

3) Now watch what it tells us in this next verse of John 1:14, watch closely now.

John 1:14

And the word was made flesh, and dwelt among us. (And we beheld his glory, The glory as of the only begotten of the father,) Full of Grace and Truth.

Now did it not say in the last part of John 4:24?

"And they that worship him must worship him in spirit and truth."

JESUS was that word that was made flesh. Why did God do that? There are two reasons that are given and I will get to the second one shortly. Here's the first:

John 3:16
For GOD so Loved the world, that he gave his only begotten Son, that

whosoever believeth in him should not perish, but have everlasting life.

John 3:17
For GOD sent not his Son into the world to condemn the world; but that the world through him might be saved.

John 3:18

He that believeth on him is not condemned: but he that believeth not is condemned already, because he hath not believed in the name of the only begotten Son of GOD.

John 3:34

For he whom GOD hath sent speaketh the words of GOD: for GOD giveth not the spirit by measure unto him.

You see, Jesus didn't come to make a name for himself, He was the messenger of GOD doing the will of the Father.
JESUS carried the Spirit of GOD within himself. JESUS had the full measure of spirit.

1 Timothy 3:16
And without controversy great is the mystery of GODLINESS: <u>GOD was manifest in the flesh,</u> Justified in the Spirit, Seen of the Angels, Preached unto the gentiles, Believed on in the world, received up into Glory.

It's so simple, yet over 2,000 years ago, the people rejected Jesus

Christ and GOD too.
Why should we be any
different? Is it not just
our insanity and our
ignorance as humans
to be the same way!?!
It's time to wake up!

John 5:22,23
For the Father judgeth
no man, but hath
committed all
judgment unto the Son:
That all men should
honour the Son, even as

*they honour the Father.
He that honoureth not
the Son honoureth not
the Father which hath
sent him.*

John 5:37

*And the Father himself,
which hath sent me,
hath borne witness of
me. Ye have neither
heard his voice at any
time, nor seen his
shape.*

John 5:38
And ye have not his word abiding in you: for whom he hath sent, him ye believe not.

Those are very powerful portions of scripture coming from both GOD and JESUS, and to think that the Jews sought to kill him...

John 5:39
Search the scriptures;for in them ye think ye have eternal life: and they are they which testify of me.

John 5:40-42
And ye will not come to me, that ye might have life.

John 5:41
I receive not honour from men.

John 5:42
But I know you, that ye have not the Love of GOD in you.

That's as subtle as it gets and that is the first reason. The second reason was a fulfillment of prophecy and the introduction of a new covenant by the Father that is laid out and explained in the book

of Hebrews. We will
start in chapter 8.

Hebrews 8:7

*For if that first covenant had
been faultless, then should
no place have been sought for
the second.*

Hebrews 8:8

*For finding fault with them,
he saith, Behold, the days
come, saith the Lord, when I
will make a new covenant
with the house of Israel and
with the house of Judah:*

Hebrews 8:9

Not according to the that I made with their fathers in the day when I took them by the hand to lead them out of Egypt; because they continued not in my covenant, and I regarded them not, saith the Lord.

Hebrews 8:10

For this is the covenant that I will make with the house of Israel after those days, saith the Lord; I will put my laws into their mind, and write them in their hearts: and I will be to them a God, and they shall be to me a people:

Hebrews 8:11

And they shall not teach every man his neighbor, and every man his brother, saying, Know the Lord: for all shall know me, from the least to the to the greatest.

Hebrews 8:12

For I will be merciful to their unrighteousness, and their sins and their iniquities will I remember no more.

Hebrews 8:13

In that he saith, A new covenant, he hath made the first old. Now that which decayeth and waxeth old is ready to vanish away.

This is the old covenant which was done away with,

and if that were not true, we would still be offering blood sacrifices from rams, goats, and bullocks. The Fathers Ten Commandments are still in effect because Jesus tells us so in the book of John.

The New covenant

Hebrews 7:22

By so much was JESUS made a surety of a better testament.

Because the Aaronic priests died: Christ ever liveth.

Hebrews 7:23

And they truly were many priests, because they were not suffered to continue by reason of death:

Hebrews 7:24

Because this man,(JESUS) because he continueth ever, hath an unchangeable priesthood.

Hebrews 7:25

Wherefore he is able also to save them to the uttermost that come unto GOD by him, seeing he ever liveth to make intercession for them.

Because Christ mediates a better covenant.

Hebrews 8:6

But now hath he obtained a more excellent ministry, by how much also he is the mediator of a better covenant, which was established upon better promises.

The Sanctuary, and sacrifice of the new covenant are realities.

Hebrews 9:11

But Christ being come an high priest of good things to come, by a greater and more perfect tabernacle, not made with hands, that is to say, not of this building;

Hebrews 9:12

Neither by the blood of goats and calves, but by his own blood he entered in once into the holy place, having obtained eternal redemption for us.

Hebrews 9:13

For if the blood of bulls and of goats, and the ashes of an heifer sprinkling the unclean, sanctifieth to the purifying of the flesh:

Hebrews 9:14

How much more shall the blood of Christ, who through the eternal Spirit offered himself without spot to GOD, purge your conscience from dead works to serve the living GOD?

Hebrews 9:15

And for this cause he is the mediator of the new testament, that by means of death, for the redemption of the transgressions that were under the first testament, they which are called might receive the promise of eternal inheritance.

The new covenant is also the last will and testament of Christ, sealed by his blood.

Hebrews 9:16

For where a testament is, there must also of necessity be the death of the testator.

Hebrews 9:17

For a testament is of force after men are dead: otherwise it is of no strength at all while the testator liveth.

Hebrews 9:18

Whereupon neither the first testament was dedicated without blood.

In these next verses, I will paraphrase, Moses had to sacrifice the bulls and goats and go through the ritual of sprinkling the tabernacle

and all the vessels, the book and all the people. And in verse 22;

Hebrews 9:22

And almost all things are by the law purged with blood; and without the shedding of blood is no remission.

Hebrews 9:23

It was therefore necessary that the patterns of things in the heavens should be purified with these; but the heavenly things themselves with better sacrifices than these.

Hebrews 9:24

For Christ is not entered into the holy places made with hands, which are figures of the true; but into heaven itself, now to appear in the presence of GOD for us:

The one sacrifice of the new covenant is better than the many sacrifices of the old.

Hebrews 9:25

Nor yet that he should offer himself often, as the high priest entereth into the holy place every year with blood of others;

Hebrews 9:26

For then must he often suffered since the foundation of the world: but now once in the end in the world hath he appeared to put away sin by the sacrifice of himself.

Hebrews 9:27

And as it is appointed unto men once to die, but after this the judgment:

Hebrews 9:28

So Christ was once offered to bear the sins of many; and unto them that look for him shall he appear the second time without sin unto salvation.

So there you have it the facts of GOD and JESUS and how the two of them brought in the new

covenant together. There is a lot more to this and later in the book I will be explaining some more of this and how it plays in with the walk of a new life in sobriety with the Lord.

You see, God and JESUS share in so much, the spirits of Grace, Mercy, Truth, Honor, Peace, Love, Repentance, Forgiveness, Faith, Righteousness, Wisdom, Commitment, Life, and Glory.

And to think that the people had JESUS put to death for no cause. Pride, Narrow-mindedness, deaf, No comprehension, oblivious to knowledge and wisdom, goodness, all the feeding and healing of the people only for the people of this world to fulfill their own self-will with the lusts of the world.

Some will hear and some will not hear and that is prophecy being fulfilled. Seems to me though... as I write this book, to live by the Lord's Commandments and walk humbly before him, it is a peaceful and fulfilling walk better than any drug or drink. Since we live in the flesh on this earth, we do not walk after the flesh pursuing our lustful desires. So we do not seek the lusts of this world. We lay down our life... We surrender to the Lord's Will. WE begin our walk in the spiritual path which entails Love, Hope, Peace, Faith,

Joy, Happiness. These are the rewards of walking in the belief of JESUS CHRIST and keeping the Fathers Commandments. For that my Brothers and Sisters, they shall dwell with you. If you don't think the blessings they offer are worth it, then you haven't lived a sincere life for them. That Love and peace and joy and faith and hope are incredibly indescribable. So my question to you is this: With all that I have explained to you, If you died today, do you know that you would go to heaven?

Isn't it time to start making mature decisions?

After all, our program of recovery needs a power greater than ourselves.

Why not let Jesus Christ in your life? He made the ultimate sacrifice of laying down his life for you. What was so wrong with him that we fail miserably to honor him? Even after God explained him to us in the Bible, we choose such a sickening ignorance of truth.

We honor dead men's final requests who haven't done near as much or anything in comparison, and yet we despise him out of our own stupidity.

We glorify movie stars and material possessions, and for what?

In the end it will avail you a big fat nothing!

GOD gave his son in unison out of LOVE...True Love.

It pains my heart to have to write about the denial of the Son. I pray for Hope for you and all who read this that you may come to the truth and awaken to his goodness if you haven't already.

1 John 5:7

For there are three that bear record in heaven, The Father, The Word, and the Holy Ghost: And these three are one.

1 John 5:8

And there are three that bear witness in earth, The Spirit, and the Water, and the Blood: and these three agree in one.

1 John 5:9

If we receive the witness of men, the witness of GOD is greater: for this is the witness of GOD which he testified of his Son.

1 John 5:10

He that believeth on the Son of GOD hath the witness in himself: he that believeth not GOD hath made him a liar; because he believeth not the record that GOD gave his Son.

1 John 5:11

And this is the record, that GOD hath given to us eternal life, and this life is in his Son.

As the author of this book, it is put on my heart that you might come to know our Lord and Savior JESUS CHRIST and that you might confess your sins. All you have to do is ask him to come into your heart. I asked at age 11, but I didn't follow the LORD's ways.

Self-will and self-seeking ways, looking to the pleasures and lusts of the world. Living by my own means and not walking in any faith what so ever. What do I have to show for my life in all my 35 years of drinking and smoking pot? Absolutely nothing but a big pile of wreckage. My LORD is patient and forgiving and he has a plan for me.

We need to understand that "humility" is a key element in our recovery and our deliverance from these bonds of addiction. When we honestly and sincerely come to terms with humility and acknowledge the fact that we have lived our life according to the wrong guidelines or principles, then we can have hope and the beginning of peace. Until you realize that, you have nothing.

Footprints

One night a man had a dream. He dreamed he was walking along the beach with the Lord. Across the sky flashed scenes from his life. For each scene, he noticed two sets of footprints in the sand; one belonged to him, and the other to the Lord.

When the last scene of his life flashed before him, he looked back at the footprints in the sand. He noticed that many times along the path of his life there was only one set of footprints. He noticed that it happened at the very lowest and saddest times in his life. This really bothered him and he questioned the Lord about it. "Lord, You said that once I decided to follow you, you'd walk with me all the way. But I have noticed that during the most troublesome times in my life, there is only one set of footprints. I don't understand why when I needed you most you would leave me." The Lord replied, "My precious, precious child, I Love you and would never leave you. During your times of trial and suffering, when you see only one set of footprints, it was then that I carried you."

Chapter 3

Now that we know...

Many are called, but few are chosen. Why is this you may ask? Human Pride and Lack of Wisdom and knowledge. Complete and total ignorance.

If we accept our calling, more of life will take on new meaning, GOD'S word takes on new levels of sense and beauty as our hearts are opened to a new life. New forms of peace will overtake us, a new desire to experience an even greater closeness with GOD and his Son JESUS CHRIST.

When I came into the VA rehab, I only wanted to crawl under a rock and disappear. Mentally, emotionally, spiritually bankrupt. I was homeless and tired of life. Life had lost all meaning, I had lost our home, my marriage, and I had abandoned my children. Jobs were being lost as fast as I could find them. I had no will left in me; my spirit was broke and I was withering fast. I knew that something was wrong with me and I had a desire to be locked up in a state hospital where I didn't have to deal with life. Not a fun place to be. I will take you back about a year or so to let you see in a general way the events that led me to the condition I ended up in. After the home loss and the separation, I moved and had a small efficiency apartment. I moved out of there and in with a friend since his father had passed away recently. We took in another roommate and we had all talked about combining our artistic talents and coming up with some new products. Well we all made like hermits and kept to ourselves, even the shoveling of a housing community; I couldn't keep up with due to my lungs and health problems. My roommate didn't really understand and I did not know at the time that I had COPD and chronic bronchitis. A bit of resentment from the roommate and I felt miserable because it felt like I had let him down. I could still help drink the beer and the whiskey and I always had a stash of pot. Come springtime and early summer; I was working to finish an orchard job and some land clearing and then that job was done. My other job of working as a vendor was taking major financial hits every month just about. I was down to the minimum of what I could make and survive. I figured since I was moving all the family's belongings out to them, I would scout out Western PA and hook up with my friends from the navy. I had a few jobs lined up along with a campsite to live at. How hard could it be to earn

$400-$600 a month and be able to party? And survive? Well… jobs were running out as the downturn in the economy affected those areas too. I was running out of money to fix the holes in the trailer. I had no running water, minimal electric; I was about out of money and eating about four times a week. I found one job that paid about $75 a week and that was making firewood. It wasn't enough and barely covered my gas expense, 1-2 meals and maybe a 12 pack. Mentally and emotionally, it was taking its toll on me. Since leaving Michigan, the Lord has been guiding me in a way yet unseen by me during this time. I was only 2 hours away from my family and the Lord said, That's not close enough. The wife rescued me financially a couple of times so I could eat and get around so that I wasn't completely stranded. I humbled myself and did ask if I could come home.

Mentally and emotionally, I was still a wreck. My wife consented to it and I half-heartedly looked for work. Who was going to hire someone that felt like a complete derelict in life? My hair was long and I had a full beard, I was 40 pounds underweight and I looked pretty rough. I found a cleaning job and that lasted about four weeks. I was guided to the VA in Bath, New York. I cried for a couple of hours wanting help just to get the courage up to walk up the stairs to the hospital. I went to the Mental Health unit and told them I was ready to be committed and committed I was. Once again I had separated myself from my family and I tried to explain to my children that Daddy needed some help. I was very much a wreck. I wanted to place the blame on all the events and people that had been a part of my life in the last few years. I wanted to blame the Navy for all my physical ailments. I of course was just the victim. (Yeah, Right!) How wrong I was! Little did I know that the Lord had me exactly where he wanted me. The VA Dom is like the Lord's house, it is a place of rest from the turmoil and trials of the world that we have let beat us down, chew us up and spit us back out again. Comes a time when we shut down and say enough is enough. I felt guilty about taking a six month break from life, because most people normal or sick don't usually get that luxury or blessing if you will. When we deny that gift given by the LORD, people get thrown out of the VA for stupidity and turning to the ways of addiction yet again! The consequence we are given is right back into the same mess and stress that we came there with and then add some more to it.

So my friends, we must surrender our worldly life and our ways, our lustful desires and actions. We accept the humility before us so we can develop our faith and trust. For our new walk is a personal one. Our walk will be a new found journey. The Spirit of the Lord will teach and guide us only if we let it. If we are up to no good, a no good spirit will be around. We make sure that we are seeking God's will for our lives. We study, we pray, we live by the Lord's Commandments.

This for me is just a portion of what I do to maintain my life. In this past year, I have a life that is unfolding before my eyes and a ministry that is being born. A new breath of life have I been given. Financially, I am a poor man that receives $126.00 per month and I still have peace and happiness from the turmoil in the world. I have my own personal teachers in my

King James Bible. They speak to me daily and help to guide me. Some will say the bible is full of contradictions or it has been changed by man over the years. These are the people who don't have a pure heart and they lack understanding and wisdom. They are proud and arrogant, walking a corrupt path and trying to lead people astray because they understand not and they are blind to the truth. You really think GOD would let his instructions be changed? Do the people think that they know better than GOD? Excuse me while I laugh to hysteria! If we want freedom from the captivity of addiction and alcoholism along with freedom from the world, this is the path that leads to life.

1 Corinthians 15:34

Awake to righteousness and sin not; For some have not

the knowledge of GOD: I speak this to your shame.

In these next verses, it tells us how we are to live our new life or the life that we should have been living all along. In 1 Corinthians chapter 13, commonly known as the "LOVE" chapter. This teaches us how to live our life and I will show you how the example plays out. GOD and JESUS talk about charity in this chapter and in essence Charity is LOVE, Starting at

1 Corinthians 13:4

GOD suffereth long, JESUS suffereth long, **Your Name** *suffereth long.*

GOD is Kind, JESUS is Kind, **Your Name** *is Kind.*

GOD envieth not, JESUS envieth not, **Your Name** *envieth not.*

GOD vaunteth not himself, JESUS vaunteth not himself, **Your Name** *vaunteth not himself.*

GOD is not puffed up, JESUS is not puffed up, **<u>Your Name</u>** *is not puffed up.*

GOD does not behave himself unseemingly, JESUS does not behave himself unseemingly, **<u>Your name</u>** *does not behave himself unseemingly.*

Love seeketh not her own.

<u>(Don't be so full of yourself.)</u>

Love faileth not.

<u>Walk in Love and you won't fail either.</u>

GOD *is not easily provoked,*
JESUS is not easily
provoked, **Your Name** *is not*
easily provoked.

GOD *thinketh no evil, JESUS*
thinketh no evil, **Your Name**
thinketh no evil.

GOD *rejoiceth not in*
iniquity, JESUS rejoiceth not
in iniquity, **Your Name**
rejoiceth not in iniquity.

GOD *rejoices in the truth,*
JESUS rejoices in the truth,
Your Name *rejoices in the*
truth.

GOD beareth all things,
JESUS beareth all things,
Your Name *beareth all things.*

GOD believeth all things,
JESUS believeth all things,
Your Name *believeth all things.*

GOD hopeth all things,
JESUS hopeth all things,
Your Name *hopeth all things.*

GOD endureth all things,
JESUS endureth all things,
Your Name *endureth all things.*

GOD never faileth, JESUS never faileth, <u>Your Name</u> never faileth.

This is how we are supposed to live our life along with GOD's Commandments, plus JESUS' teachings. Is this so difficult in life? Really? Look at the never faileth part...hard to believe, but with GOD and JESUS in our heart, we cannot fail. Look at David who killed Goliath with such a strong faith and love in GOD. A young boy facing a giant, Goliath a man of war since his youth slain by a believer of GOD. Nothing is impossible with GOD and JESUS. But in this world today in which we live, who and what are we turning to? I can tell you the list is very long and GOD and JESUS are not a part of it. We turn to the seven deadly sins and Satan's deceptions. To cope, we turn to chemicals and booze and sexual lusts to name a few. Shame on us and shame on our ignorance. I speak to you the truth, because this has been the experience in my life for 35 years. Today I have peace and deliverance from the bonds of addiction and alcoholism and true love in my heart. I have no desire to drink or use or pursue the evils of the world in ignorance and lack of maturity. Use your gift of sight to study for yourself, open your heart because your ways and beliefs have not done you much good.

Proverbs 2:11

Let us use some discretion, for it shall preserve thee, understanding shall keep thee.

I had to do this at the VA, I humbled myself and took on a thought process and determination to get to the basics of who GOD and JESUS truly are. I learned about the love and grace and mercy and forgiveness. I learned about faith and hope. I learned about my emotional triggers and my coping processes, I learned most about acceptance. I seen my improper thought processes and I was able to develop new ones, thanks to the Lord. This was a beautiful time in my life, because of the opportunity to examine my life and see where I went wrong in life. This too, was one of the greatest awakenings I have ever experienced in my life. The abundant mercy and grace that was bestowed upon me. I have to say that I took it upon myself the mindset of the shepherd boy David, a young man after GOD'S own heart who would settle for nothing less. After 35 years of trying to do myself in, I accepted my humility, my defeat of trying to live life on the world's terms and it just does not work. That is a big pill to swallow. It is like a great burden lifted off the shoulders and the heart and the mind when we come to this awareness. As addicts and alcoholics, we need to live our life in a completely different fashion completely with no reservation or apprehension. Our life depends on this. We don't go back to old friends that use and drink, we don't go back to old neighborhoods. When I got out of the VA, 90% of those that discharged within a 3-4 week period went right back to their old sick ways. Why? They had not the Fear of the Lord in their heart. They had no application of the program materials in their life and they were still stuck on ignorantly relying on one's own self. They failed to surrender their life to our Lord and Saviour JESUS CHRIST! These are the people who could talk the talk, but failed to walk the walk.

Hebrews 10:19

Having therefore, brethren, boldness to into the holiest by the blood of JESUS,

Hebrews 10:20

By a new and living way, which he hath consecrated for us, through the veil, that is to say, his flesh,

Hebrews 10:21

And having a high priest over the house of GOD;

Hebrews 10:22

Let us draw near with a true heart in full assurance of faith, having our hearts sprinkled from an evil conscience, and our bodies washed with pure water:

Hebrews 10:23

Let us hold fast the profession of faith without wavering; (For he is faithful that promised;)

Hebrews 10:24

And let us consider one another to provoke unto love and to good works:

Hebrews 10:25

Not forsaking the assembling of ourselves together, as the manner of some is; but exhorting one another: and so much the more, as ye see the day approaching.

The day is coming and fast approaching! That bit of scripture above is applied to our life and accepting JESUS CHRIST in our life and helping one another along the path of a spiritual walk.

I've noticed too that when we walk in our new life, our perception begins to change as we start to grow and mature. I used to have hair down to the middle of my back and a big bushy beard. I was referred to as JESUS CHRIST most of the time. I thought this was a great thing and used to tell everyone to keep that thought. I was so full of myself that I didn't see the underlying message for 10 months, it was the spirit telling me to walk like CHRIST. My pastor talked to me about my hair and beard and I thought I had a ministry to perform while looking the part. But... My hair and my beard were only covering up the shame and guilt I carried. That was another dose of humility and that was OK, because it showed me so much more. I'm glad I've got JESUS CHRIST in my life, he allows me to learn and smiles when I get it right and still loves me even when I don't. So let us walk humbly with our hearts, ears and eyes open all the while keeping the Father's commandments in our hearts and walk according to them. Let us not be of them that are in the poem on the next page...

So Blind…So Ignorant…

Is the most of what we see,
How much we miss.
Of God's mercy and his love that could be,
Because of an excuse and choice made by man,
So blind…so ignorant…and possibly damned

To the life given freely as long as we believe,
In a man called Jesus,
God's son you see.

But man is blind…so ignorant…you see,
We criticize the word, inspired by God and Jesus
And trusted to man.
All the writings of the apostles: disciples and prophets,
Were gifts to us from "I am"

To give simple basic instructions,
Of how to live towards one another,
And on the Earth,
Knowing the key points of God and Jesus and such.

So blind…so ignorant…
Are we to this beauty?
That we choose to do Satan's folly,
And hold God and Jesus in disgust

A Minister of God

Chapter 4

Into the steps...

Step 1

We admitted we were powerless, that our lives had become unmanageable.

Note the two phrases of the first sentence

"We admitted"- To start with...

So now this is not a do it yourself program, the term "We" are those who have

gone before you. It is also a fact that we have others to talk with who will help us along the way.

"Admitted"

We made a confession that there is a problem. This is a beginning of honesty. It is also a humbling step as well as a surrendering of our life. Let us not forget that "Admitted is an action word, and it is a very crucial step in the realm of honesty. It is a step that helps to prepare our minds and our heart to start afresh. It is the confession and done with willingness asking GOD to come into our heart that purifies our heart to begin a change.

Now let's move on to "We were Powerless"

People that are of the worldly ways think they have power and it is a standard norm or a stigma of a false belief of society in the world. Everyone claims a strong dis-belief and shuns powerlessness. Those who don't show powerlessness are those who have not a pure heart, nor do they walk humbly with the LORD, their sobriety will not last, nor will it be of any quality because of pride, ego and self-will and ignorance of dis-belief which is nothing more than fear. The realization of powerlessness means to lose control; we have become bankrupt in

many areas of our lives…
mainly mentally, physically
and spiritually. We are
suffering the consequences
of sin. We have continued
down one of Satan's paths
and he doesn't have to lift a
finger because man is so
haughty and corrupt in our
ways already that we
continue to kill ourselves
with ignorance and
stupidity by shoving foreign
substances into our body
which shouldn't be put
there to begin with. We

think we're cool, we think we're entitled, and that is so far from the truth!! We have been deceived and we continue to deceive ourselves. It is time to awaken brothers and sisters! It is time to become free from the bonds of addiction. When you walk in the ways of the one true GOD, you no longer suffer the weight of the burden of worldly ways, you become free. You must continue to walk in GOD'S ways and study and pray.

You will be faced with Satan's attacks of temptation and this is just a fact of life. However, if we are keeping the Father's commandments, It will be much easier to discern right from wrong. You can't be praying one minute and swearing up a storm the next to just hang with the friends, you may want to consider what a friend truly is and surround yourself with people in your life who share those same values to walk that path of goodness and not of corruptness. If you have a problem with swearing, then you need to take it to the Lord in prayer because no man can tame the tongue, we ask the Lord to do this for us and we practice restraint. Every time you catch yourself, you ask for forgiveness and start again afresh. I'm not perfect at this, but these are the principles and precepts I live by. I still struggle with this in certain areas; the game of horseshoes is/are still a challenge for me and a few words slip every time I miss the stake. So... I don't play as often as I would like to. This is a form of self-discipline and it is something you will use in your new walk if you are indeed serious.

Being powerless is a wonderful journey when we grasp that concept of walking and trusting in the Lord. You see we don't walk around like a bunch of zombies or so-called JESUS freaks. Today we are living for the truth, we help those in need... we help those who are lost due to the evils of the world find their way back to JESUS CHRIST. We help the hungry, the fatherless, and the widows. We get together with our church groups to help grow the church for our Lord and Saviour first and foremost. My church is aware of my alcoholism and addiction struggles. So my church would like me to start a Reformers Unanimous group run through the church. It is an addiction therapy group that involves teaching, learning, listening and doing. Being accountable and helping others, that is what we are supposed to be doing. There is a new hope and a new life when we lay down our old ways and our old life and it is a greater satisfaction than any stupid drug can ever

give to you. Surrendering your life means this...

1 Peter 2:1

Wherefore laying aside all malice, and all guile, and hypocrisies, and envies, and all evil speakings,

1 Peter 2:2

As newborn babes, desire the sincere milk of the word, that ye may grow thereby:

1 Peter 2:3

If so be ye have tasted that the Lord is gracious.

1 Peter 2:4

To whom coming, as unto a living stone, disallowed indeed of men, but chosen of GOD, and precious,

1 Peter 2:5

Ye also, as lively stones, are built up a spiritual house, an holy priesthood, to offer up spiritual sacrifices, acceptable to GOD by JESUS CHRIST.

1 Peter 2:6

Wherefore also it is contained in the scripture, Behold I lay in Sion a chief corner stone, elect, precious: and he that believeth on him shall not be confounded.

1 Peter 2:7

Unto you therefore which believe he is precious: but unto them which be disobedient, the stone which the builders disallowed, the same is made the head of the corner,

1 Peter 2:8

And a stone of stumbling, and a rock of offence, even to them which stumble at the word, being disobedient: whereunto also they were appointed.

Is it so wrong to live a righteous life? Don't you owe it to yourself, the Father, and the SON? Brothers and sisters, we have entered into the end times, the world is going to see much more evil. Do you wish to be a part of that misery and insanity? Or do you want to be protected from it?

Nine things to consider

We have to be 100% convinced that we have a problem.

All of us have mental issues to some varying degree which require additional counseling and that's ok, so long as we acknowledge those issues and ask for some help.

You have to want sobriety, and put your all into it with no reservations or expectations.

True change takes true effort.

If while in treatment, your life... continues to fall apart around you, don't be alarmed, it is just the wreckage of our life catching up with us.

Keep in mind, GOD speaks with his spirit through our heart, feelings, and emotions.

My brothers and sisters, keep GOD first in your life.

Those who reject the gift of recovery are given back into captivity and the increased insanity of the addiction.

Those who walk with hidden fears when they are discharged aren't right with GOD and will drink/use again within hours of leaving the facility.

Chapter 5

Step 2

Came to believe that a power greater than ourselves,such as Jesus could restore us to sanity.

That power is GOD and his Son, Lord JESUS CHRIST our Saviour. As I've stated before in this book and asked "How many of you want to keep doing it by the ways of man?" and displaying ignorance toward GOD and JESUS?

Someday you will have to give an account of your life to him.

How many more rehabs and institutions will you use and waste the time of the counselors and staff? You just might be taking up space and robbing someone else of the opportunity that is really serious about getting well. You will have to give an account for that too. So when will you learn? You do 28 days or 3 months or 6 months? Where is God and JESUS in all of this? If you relapsed, you weren't doing his will! Maybe you should go back and study chapter 1 again with an open heart. Both steps 1 and 2 are study steps. Step 1 allows you to see the magnitude of your problem and step 2 allows you to see the Saviour who is going to help you if you let him. Once we realize the truth and fact that we that we can't do this on our own...When that truth comes, don't wait to ask JESUS into your life. If you can also realize that we are at war with evil and corruptions of this world, our addiction/alcoholism are but mere petty symptoms of the underlying issue. When we see it in this light, hope will manifest herself and open ways to some new doors for you to knock on. I can tell you that I don't go a relaps'n because I believe in my Lord and Saviour, I have faith and trust in him. I also know the consequences for turning my back on him and going and doing my own thing. I am too much a chicken to provoke my Lord to anger. You really have to ask yourself... "Where did I get my beliefs?" Did it come from religion? Remember, religion is man-made and does not usually reflect GOD'S truth or GOD'S Doctrine. Did you half-heartedly study GOD in the past? Does your church preach the gospel of

JESUS CHRIST? Do they offer altar calls? Remember these are study steps and the questions you need to get answers to are these types. I want you to be able to overcome the world, and not be confounded.

The spiritual side of step 2 is having Hope and getting to know who GOD really is. This is so important because you don't want just anybody working on your heart, you want someone who is qualified, preferably factory direct from heaven. You want someone to mend the spirit and to give you a life that is really worth living. JESUS can do this and he's open 24/7. Just think he can adjust your mind and install an upgrade and there isn't any hidden fee's or charges.

Chapter 6

Step 3

Made a decision to turn our will and our life over to the care of GOD and Jesus as we understand him.

It is my responsibility to help assist you in the truth, in the phrase "as we understand him" why not start with the portion of scripture from 1 Corinthians chapter 13 from chapter 3 of this book. Making this decision is a big step but it is also a step in the right direction. It's a mature decision that you can smile about because you will have peace if you do it right. Please don't make the mistake of choosing an inanimate object like a door knob like it's sometimes suggested. That becomes idolatry. Choosing JESUS CHRIST will get you the gift of eternal life. Helping

others along to work through these steps will get you a crown of Glory.

1 Peter 5:1

The elders which are among you I exhort, who am also an elder, and a witness of the sufferings of Christ, and also a partaker of the glory that shall be revealed

1 Peter 5:2

Feed the flock of GOD which is among you, taking the oversight thereof, not by constraint, but willingly; not for filthy lucre, but of a ready mind;

1 Peter 5:3

Neither as being lord's over God's heritage, but being ensamples to the flock.

1 Peter 5:4

And when the Chief Shepherd shall appear, ye shall receive a Crown of Glory that fadeth not away.

1 Peter 5:5

Likewise, ye younger, submit yourselves unto the elder. Yea, all of you be subject one to another, and be clothed with humility: For GOD resisteth the proud, and giveth grace to the humble.

1 Peter 5:6

Humble yourselves therefore under the mighty hand of GOD, that he may exalt you in due time:

1 Peter 5:7

Casting all your care upon him; for he careth for you.

1 Peter 5:8

Be sober, be vigilant; because your adversary the

devil, as a roaring lion, walketh about, seeking whom he may devour:

1 Peter 5:9

Whom resist stedfast in the faith, knowing that the same afflictions are accomplished in your brethren that are in the world.

1 Peter 5:10

But let the GOD of all grace, who hath called us unto his eternal glory by JESUS CHRIST, after that ye have suffered a while, make you perfect, stablish, strengthen, settle you.

1 Peter 5:11

To him be glory and dominion for ever and ever. Amen.

Boy if that doesn't say it all. Sounds like a twelve step meeting straight from

the bible along with a very nice reward and the only other difference is this one has a Chief Shepherd, bet you can't guess who? It is Jesus. You see it is our duty as men and women to help feed the flock and be the examples. We share our experience, strength and hope. We are not put in authority positions in the groups. We are to be sober and vigilant, not consumed with the ways of the world and our lustful desires. The only thing the world has to offer is a hospital bed or a grave. I'll take the crown. This step is a very important one and that involves surrendering your life to Jesus. God gave us free will to choose, the correct choice is to follow God's ways. Imagine if everyone in the world chose God's ways? The world would be a completely different place. Why people refuse to surrender...Lack of knowledge, Lack of study, Wrong information and an attitude to boot as a result of laziness. It is our own self-will or freedom of choice that works against us in an instant to stifle anything because of our attitude.

That is why our lives are in such chaos. Do you see how evil-minded we are?

We are like the spoiled kid that gets what he

wants, when he wants and at all cost just to shut him up or you will hear whining and the poor me syndrome. There is absolutely no discipline there. There is no self-control. There is only selfish desire and I want, I

want, I want. This is what we need to surrender, because it is not doing anyone a bit of good. Just how do we surrender? We humble our self and pray to Jesus and ask for forgiveness. It's that simple. Just make sure your heart is sincere. Every time you here about Jesus, that's an invitation or a calling if you will. We are all chosen, look at what transpired when he chose his disciples, they dropped everything and followed him. Now are we perfect at this, dropping everything and following him? Not by a long shot unless you are going to be a missionary full time, then you may have a chance. The world unfortunately and our society don't mesh with these ideas. So what's the point you may wonder? We still need to surrender our ways and follow the Lord's ways best that we can. We need to trust that he will provide a way for us; we need to believe and continue studying. We study about things of our new life, grace, faith, truth, honesty, wisdom, knowledge and understanding to name a few.

Remember we are making a decision to turn our will and our life over to the care of GOD as we understand him. We are seeking his guidance because our ways have not produced much good.

Ecclesiastes 12:13

Let us hear the conclusion of the whole matter: Fear

GOD, *and keep his commandments: for this is the whole duty of man.*

Ecclesiastes 12:14

For GOD shall bring every work into judgment, with every secret thing, whether it be good, or whether it be evil.

I think all of us are tired of the hangovers and

lifestyles that we lead and if you are in a treatment center, here's a verse for you.

1 Peter 4:17

For the time is come that judgment must begin at the house of GOD: And if it first begin at us, what shall be the end of them that obey not the gospel of GOD.

If you are in a rehab, that is a time of rest. I look at it while I was in the VA and it was time for my judgment along with a time to examine my past life, to study and see who God truly is and what I have been missing out on. His blessings are wonderful and beyond comprehension unless you have JESUS in your life, you won't experience them.

Chapter 7

Wanting to change

Step 4

Made a searching and fearless moral inventory of ourself, because we needed it.

True change begins from a desire within our self, an honest sincerity to mend our ways. GOD and JESUS are knocking on

our heart for us to awaken and clean up our act and clean all the secrets and dirty laundry out of our closet. We need to do a lot of writing about our actions and we need to be truthful. What we don't say is it's all right here in my head, that's procrastination and deceit for fear and laziness, this gets reflected in our attitude of old behavior or fear of success or you fear being obedient to the Lord because you already have a 1,000 excuses as to why it won't work. What you might fail to understand is that even though you may be working the steps in a singular fashion in the beginning, later on you will be working different steps on different subject matter. For those of you who have significant others, you may be ready to forgive and forget and start over with the amends portion showing through in your sincereness and your actions. I was convinced that I didn't Love my wife correctly the way GOD and JESUS had intended. I was absolutely correct and dead on. I was following the ways of the world of man's mis-directed notions. Man being head of the house and ruler over all that she does so that man can go and do what he pleases. What a bunch of malarkey! So we can be the macho boss inflated with false ego and pride. When in fact we need to be catering to their needs! I discovered that when I am irritated at my wife and some of the things she does, I need to step up to the plate and ask or offer to do things for her that I normally wouldn't do as the macho idiot. In the Bible it tells us to treat our wives as we would treat a weaker vessel. If we have a weaker vessel, we treat it with extra tender loving care! Not condescending, or belittling or inferior. Got that? May I remind you or teach you that GOD used Wisdom in a very unique way. First we must understand wisdom.

Proverbs 3:13

Happy is the man that findeth wisdom, and the man that getteth understanding.

Proverbs 3:14

For the merchandise of it is better than the merchandise of silver, and the gain thereof than fine gold.

Proverbs 3:15

She is more precious than rubies: and all the things thou canst desire are not to be compared unto her.

Proverbs 3:16

Length of days is in her right hand; and in her left hand riches and honour.

Proverbs 3:17

Her ways are ways of pleasantness, and all her paths are peace.

Proverbs 3:18

She is a tree of life to them that lay hold on her: and happy is every one that retaineth her.

Proverbs 3:19

The Lord by wisdom hath founded the earth; by understanding hath he established the heavens.

Now watch the references in this next set of verses, JESUS is speaking...

Proverbs 4:1

Hear, ye children, the instruction of a father, and attend to know understanding.

Proverbs 4:2

For I give you good doctrine, forsake ye not my law.

Proverbs 4:3

For I was my father's son, tender and only beloved in the sight of my mother.

Proverbs 4:4

He taught me also, and said unto me, Let thine heart retain my words: keep my commandments and live.

Proverbs 4:5

Get wisdom, get understanding: forget it not; neither decline from the words of my mouth.

Proverbs 4:6

Forsake her not, and she shall preserve thee: love her, and she shall keep thee.

Proverbs 4:7

Wisdom is the principal thing; therefore get wisdom: and with all thy getting get understanding.

Proverbs 4:8

Exalt her, and she shall promote thee: she shall bring thee to honour, when thou dost embrace her.

Proverbs 4:9

She shall give to thine head an ornament of grace: a crown of glory shall she deliver unto thee.

Proverbs 4:13

Take fast hold of instruction; let her not go: keep her; for she is thy life.

So wisdom is part of the key of life, we haven't gotten to know her and experience the goodness that she has to offer. But if you do your fourth step honestly and completely, you will get to experience her peace. Now we know where our wives and mothers get their knowledge for comfort. Adam and Eve were not afforded the gift of wisdom, but JESUS was. Watch this next set of

verses and the origins of Wisdom.

Proverbs 8:1-36

Doth not wisdom cry? And understanding put forth her voice?

She standeth in the top of high places of the paths.

She crieth at the gates, at the entry of the city, at the coming in at the doors.

Unto you, O men, I call; and my voice is to the sons of man.

O ye simple, understand wisdom: and, ye fools, be ye of an understanding heart.

Hear; for I will speak of excellent things; and the opening of my lips shall be right things.

For my mouth shall speak truth; and wickedness is an abomination to my lips.

All the words of my mouth are in righteousness; there is nothing forward or perverse in them.

They are all plain to him that understandeth, and right to them that find knowledge.

Receive my instruction, and not silver; and knowledge rather than choice gold.

For wisdom is better than rubies; and all things that may be desired are not to be compared to it.

I wisdom dwell with prudence, and find out

knowledge of witty
inventions.

The fear of the Lord is to
hate evil: pride and
arrogancy, and the evil
way and the froward
mouth do I hate.

Counsel is mine, and sound
wisdom: I am
understanding; I have
strength.

By me kings reign, and
princes decree justice.

By me princes rule, and nobles, even all the judges of the earth.

I love them that love me; and those that seek me early shall find me.

Riches and honour are with me; yea, durable riches and righteousness.

My fruit is better than gold, yea, than fine gold; and my revenue than choice silver.

I lead in the way of righteousness, in the midst of the paths of judgment:

That I may cause those that love me to inherit substance; and I will fill their treasures.

The Lord possessed me in the beginning of his way, before his works of old.

I was set up from everlasting, from the beginning, or ever the earth was.

When there were no depths,
I was brought forth; when
there were no fountains
abounding with water.

Before the mountains were
settled, before the hills was
I brought forth:

While as yet he had not
made the earth, nor the
fields, nor the highest part
of the dust of the world.

When he prepared the
heavens, I was there: when
he set a compass upon the
face of the depth:

When he established the clouds above: when he strengthened the fountains of the deep:

When he gave to the sea his decree, that the waters should not pass his commandment: when he appointed the foundations of the earth:

Then I was by him, as one brought up with him: and I was his daily delight, rejoicing always before him;

Rejoicing in the habitable part of his earth; and my delights were with the sons of men.

Now therefore hearken unto me, O ye children: for blessed are they that keep my ways.

Hear instruction, and be wise, and refuse it not.

Blessed is the man that heareth me, watching daily at my gates, waiting at the posts of my doors.

For whoso findeth life, and shall obtain favour of the Lord.

But he that sinneth against me wrongeth his own soul: all they that hate me love death.

Wisdom is pretty incredible, and to think that is just one of the family.

Proverbs 9: 1-18

Wisdom hath builded her house, she hath hewn out her seven pillars;

*She hath killed her beasts;
she hath mingled her wine;
she hath also furnished her
table.*

*She hath sent forth her
maidens: she crieth upon
the highest places of the
city,*

*Whoso is simple, let him
turn in hither: as for him
that wanteth
understanding, she saith to
him,*

Come, eat of my bread, and
drink of the wine which I
have mingled.

Forsake the foolish, and
live; and go in the way of
understanding.

He that reproveth a scorner
getteth to himself shame:
and he that rebuketh a
wicked man getteth himself
a blot.

Reprove not a scorner, lest
he hate thee: rebuke a wise
man, and he will love thee.

Give instruction to a wise man, and he will be yet wiser: teach a just man, and he will increase in learning.

The fear of the Lord is the beginning of wisdom: and the knowledge of the holy is understanding.

For by me thy days shall be multiplied, and the years of thy life shall be increased.

If thou be wise, thou shalt be wise for thyself: but if

thou scornest, thou alone shalt bear it.

The Foolish woman:

A foolish woman is clamorous: she is simple, and knoweth nothing.

For she sitteth at the door of her house, on a seat in the high places of the city,

To call passengers who go right on their ways:

Whoso is simple, let him turn in hither: and as for him that wanteth understanding, she saith to him,

Stolen waters are sweet, and bread eaten in secret is pleasant.

But he knoweth not that the dead are there; and that her guests are in the depths of hell.

Get to know wisdom in this process, she is your life and I tell you all of this because it keeps me sober and clean and if we are doing our fourth step,

it won't hurt to have a good knowledge of wisdom. She makes our fourth step seem easy. So let's get to writing it all down. It allows us to see clearer the areas that need to be addressed. For myself I started with the most recent times of my life within the last 5 years. Keep in mind, just because we write it down doesn't mean we are done dealing with it. We are only writing it down to get it off of the mind because some of our issues may be severe and we have not the proper coping skills or counseling in place to effectively deal with it properly. (Thank you Skip for sharing that with me) It doesn't mean we ignore issues. You will want to be in a quiet place away from distractions. Ask in a prayer for help and guidance on this. The spirit will guide you. I look at this self-examination as a time to sort out our life and figure out just where we went wrong with the Lord's commandments in our life. How deceived were we? Our thinking was pretty backwards. On the next page, this is where we end up and how we end up. I wrote my life out on paper all the way back to about six years old and looked at everything I had ever done and the choices I made and asked myself "where did I have the Lord in all of this?" Pretty far from us.

182

It is not a pleasant place. The agony, despair, depression, anxiety, withdrawals and mostly because of fear of being who we truly are. We become lost and broken and we are downright miserable carrying all the excess baggage. In order to relieve the suffering, we ask the Lord to guide us and give us the courage to confront our issues by writing about them because they gnaw at us and drain us of our will to live. Once we get them on paper they lose their power over us because we stop giving them the power over us to hurt us. Some of my most recent topics within the last 5 years of my life. I put those on paper first because they were the fuel for my addiction and drinking. The pain I felt with these issues was very great and not a pleasant place to be. As I wrote them out I was kind of numb and I wasn't blaming and condemning others as I wrote them out. This was my confession to GOD and myself. It allowed me to see my character defects and how far from the truth I had gone and how I could justify it falsely. I could see the process of reasoning that I used. I could see just how wrong I was when in the time(s) that these issues happened. How I thought I was right and justified at that time only to see how wrong I was completely. I prayed for forgiveness and asked the Lord to teach me the truth about how I should Love my wife and children better. How I should be the father and husband that the Lord would have me to be. I was living according to the ways of the world and the false pre-conceived notions, the macho, egotistical, all inclusive in charge, dwell under my thumb! You need permission from me to do anything! What a lie... and so far from the truth! It was when I was willing and fearless that GOD removed the blindness and I was convicted, forgiven and loved. He gave me peace and wisdom and joy. I was allowed with his help to conquer fear and take a major step in Faith and belief. This is the result for trusting him and doing what I was supposed to do. A part of it comes from a desire to know GOD'S heart, just as the shepherd boy David had that same desire in the story of David and Goliath. I'll share that story with you and for me what I discovered.

ONE SHEPHERD BOY...

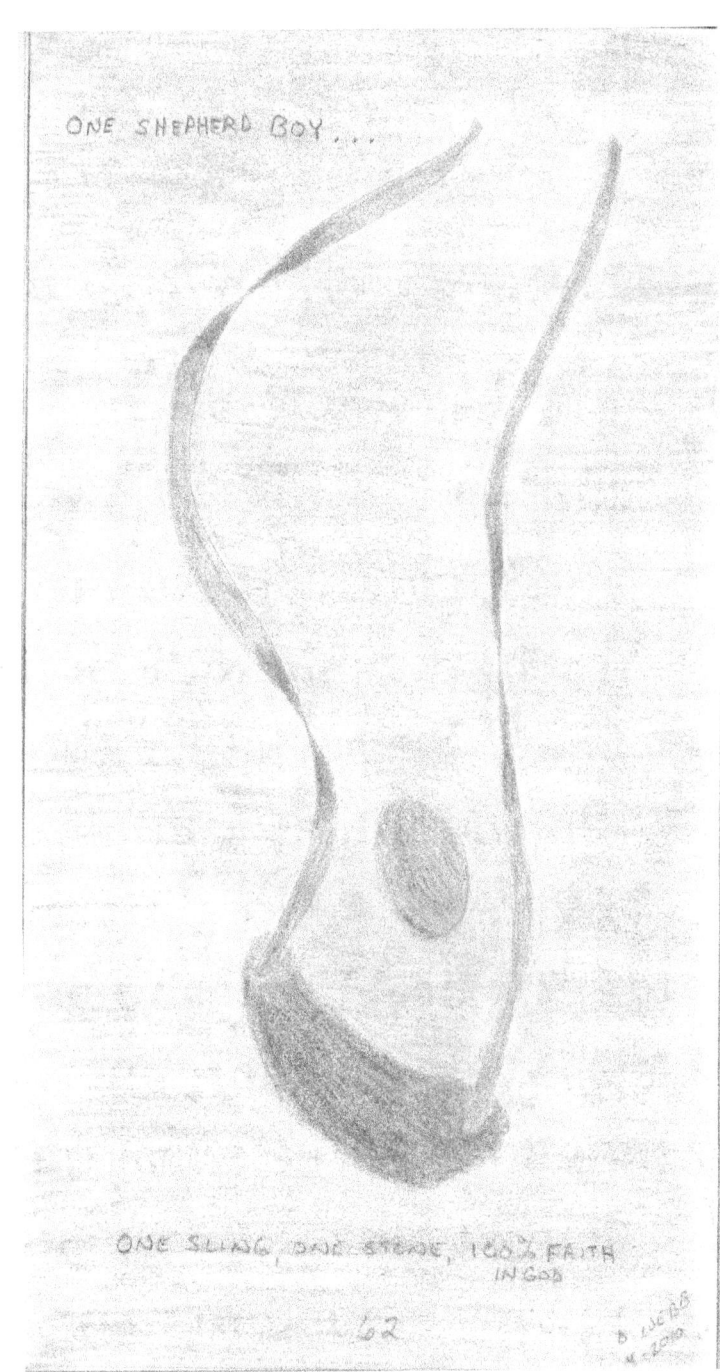

ONE SLING, ONE STONE, 100% FAITH
IN GOD

62

Chapter 8

David & Goliath & GOD

1 Samuel 17

Goliath..., sounds large and gigantic doesn't it? Much like our addiction. Goliath struck fear and intimidation into his adversaries. Not only by his physical demeanor and his layer of armor, but the largeness of his weapons that would strike a man down for good in in one blow. Goliath's sole purpose was to destroy and take captive because from the time of his youth, Goliath didn't have a care for the one true GOD. He only had a false love of the world and false pride with an arrogant ego to boot. Putting people down that would come against him or try to resist him, by using vain words and his large appearance to mentally destroy them by taking hope from them, inflicting words to lead us astray from having faith in GOD and doing what is right. Goliath conquered armies through fear and intimidation. So we fall prey to Goliath and submit ourselves to his ways thinking we will be alright only to find that those ways of Goliath have we turned them to oneself...Delivering fatal blows that take us farther down than we ever could have imagined, leaving us ragged and beaten down, wanting to die, but death would not come. Yet are we still kept alive by the love and mercy of the one true GOD, Our Lord and Saviour JESUS CHRIST.

He calls us to awaken and gives us the courage and faith to rise up and take down the beastly giant. The shepherd boy David was given this courage and faith, for when he faced Goliath, David was not alone, for GOD stood with him. David didn't focus on his older brothers' jealousy and negativity. His brothers lack of faith, nor their chastisement and accusations. For forty days Goliath issued challenges to the army of Israel for someone to come out and fight... and then here comes David, David did not give way to Goliath's insults and cursing him by a false god. Goliath tried to intimidate David yet

again, in verse 45 GOD uses humility through David when he addresses Goliath:

1 Samuel 17:45

Thou comest to me with a sword and a spear and with a shield: But I come to thee in the name of the Lord of hosts, The GOD of the armies of Israel, whom thou hast defied.

1 Samuel 17:46

This day will the Lord deliver thee into mine

hand; and I will smite thee and take thy head from thee; and I will give the carcases of the host of the philistines this day unto the fowls of the air, and to the wild beasts of the earth; that all the earth may know that there is a GOD in Israel.

1 Samuel 17:48

And it came to pass, when Goliath arose and came

and drew near to meet David, that David hastened, and ran toward the army to meet Goliath.

1 Samuel 17:49

And David took a stone and slang it, and smote Goliath in his forehead; and he fell upon his face to the earth.

So my friends, we can beat this Goliath called addiction. But let us not forget to have Faith and

Trust in GOD; or we too
can be smitten by the pipe
or the needle or the drink
or the next pill might just
be the sword we die by.

A Minister of God

This story has helped me along in recovery to keep addiction in perspective. It also reminds me to have faith and hope that with GOD I can beat this addiction. So strong a faith, such determination, willingness, fearlessness and a great obedience along with the courage. These items are essential when doing a fourth step confession or inventory. I had to look back to when I was 6 or 7 all the while asking myself "Where did I start to go wrong according to GOD'S laws and ways?" I wrote my fourth step like an auto biography or story of my life. I found out more this way and the reward has been a deeper sense of honesty, peace and a beautiful spiritual path. For some of the major events that happened in life, I wrote them out separately, until I had developed those additional coping skills that I mentioned earlier in the previous chapter. The whole beauty of this is I start to see my life unfold. It is a time of examination of our heart, mind and soul. If you are in a treatment center, this is a great time to work on this.

Chapter 9

Step 5

Admitted to GOD and Jesus, to ourselves, and to another human being the exact nature of our wrongs.

This is a disclosure step, and we need discernment when it comes to talking about our issues on the fourth step. You want someone who has experience in these matters. Your counselors, therapists, Chaplains,

Pastors, Ministers and friends that support you and you can trust. The most important part of this step is admitting to God, the second is admitting to ourselves. Some of my items was brought out at the AA and NA meetings and at the time, I was fearless and cared not who heard it. I was granted the courage to talk about it and I did. Emotions flowed from me and the Lord heard me too. He was right there with me as I went through my issues. Sometimes, people didn't even know I was working on my 5th step when I had long and close conversations of my fears and how to that I needed to forgive myself. But sharing at the meetings had a couple of points.

The first was; I had to take that step of faith and overcome fear so that I might be showing an example to my friends who might be struggling.

The second; I needed to put that issue to rest and have peace within so as to make way for the new change that comes in.

For me, that's the Lord at work in my life. You see I believe if you make it to step 5, not all of what you wrote on the fourth step can be dealt with at one time on the 5th step. That is my personal belief and I say that because you will have other issues that are easier to deal with, whereas some issues may take you longer to get through. The coping skills come into play here as I was reminded by Skip. So that's my personal thoughts on the matter. The other thought that comes to mind is trusting in the Lord that he will not give us more than we can handle. This approach allows the spirit to help us along and he will guide us through those issues if we let him.

I believe this is a more practical approach with a much greater potential for making a stronger program. It is a matter of progressing on ward and allows you some variety and flavor for the steps. It helped me to grasp the program and how it works a whole lot better. The reward for doing this;

Proverbs 2:10-12

When wisdom entereth into thine heart, and knowledge is pleasant unto the soul;

Discretion shall preserve thee, understanding shall keep thee:

To deliver thee from the way of the evil man, from the man that speaks froward things.

These verses for me are the transformation of myself from within.

Proverbs 3:13

Happy is the man that findeth wisdom, and the man that getteth understanding.

Job 28:28

And unto the man he said, Behold the Fear of the Lord, That is wisdom; and to depart from evil is understanding.

Sincerity and Honesty will yield a lot. For the change that takes place, that's beautiful beyond words or

comprehension. It is a really nice place to be. As we go through the steps and apply them in our life, our horizons will broaden. The topic of "Fear of the Lord" as I mentioned earlier has many attributes.

Proverbs 1:7-9

The Fear of the Lord is the beginning of knowledge: but fools despise wisdom and instruction.

My son hear the instruction of thy father, and forsake not the law of thy Mother:

For they shall be an ornament of grace unto thy head, and chains about thy neck.

Proverbs 3:22

So shall they be life unto thy soul, and grace to thy neck.

Chapter 10

Step 6

Were entirely ready to have GOD remove all these defects of character.

Through GOD'S grace and instruction, we are leaving our old self behind. We no longer have many of the desire's we once had. We still will be tempted by the world and Satan's ways, But not GOD, because GOD does not work in that manner. How do we know when we are ready for this step? We have become more GOD conscious for one. We have less stress, and more peace. We have just off-loaded a good portion of our issue's and gotten a good look at our character defects. Our flaws that helped in our ability to make proper decisions improperly and for all the wrong reasons. In

1 Thessalonians 1:3

Remembering without ceasing your work of faith, and labour of Love, and patience of hope in our Lord JESUS CHRIST, in the sight of GOD and our Father;

1 Thessalonians 1:4

Knowing, brethren beloved, your election of GOD.

In Colossians, It tells of the change we are going through, we seek not the things of the world.

Colossians 3:1-17

If ye then be risen with CHRIST, seek those things which are above, where CHRIST sitteth on the right hand of GOD

Set your affection on things above, not on things on the earth.

For ye are dead, and your life is hid with CHRIST in GOD.

When CHRIST who is our life, shall appear, then shall

Ye also appear with him in glory.

Mortify therefore your members which are upon the earth; fornication, uncleanness, inordinate affection, evil concupiscence, and covetnous, which is idolatry:

For which things' sake the wrath of GOD cometh on the children of disobedience:

In the which ye also walked some time, when ye lived in them.

But now ye also put off all these; anger, wrath, malice, blasphemy, filthy communication out of your mouth.

Lie not one to another, seeing that ye have put off the old man with his deeds;

And have put on the new man, which is renewed in knowledge after the image of him that created him.

When there is neither Greek or Jew, circumcision or uncircumcision, Barbarian, Scythian, Bond nor Free: But Christ is all, and in all.

Put on therefore, as the elect of GOD, holy and beloved, bowels of mercies, kindness, humbleness of mind, meekness, longsuffering;

Forbearing one another, and forgiving one another, If any man have a quarrel against any: even as CHRIST forgave you, so also do ye.

And above all these things put on charity which is the bond of perfectness.

And let the peace of GOD rule in your hearts, to the which also are ye called in one body; and be ye thankful.

Let the word of CHRIST dwell in you richly in all wisdom; teaching and admonishing one another in psalms and hymns and spiritual songs, singing with grace in your hearts to the Lord.

And whatsoever ye do in word or deed, do all in the name of the Lord JESUS, giving thanks to GOD and the Father by him.

You see brothers and sisters, our bible tell us the truth about how we used to live our lives and how we need to let go and let GOD do the leading.

He tells us that we are his elect in Colossians. He also tells us we need to focus in on mercies from within, kindness, humbleness of mind, meekness, Long suffering, Forgiveness and most of all, Love.

Romans 8:12-14

Therefore, brethren, we are debtors, not to the flesh, to live after the flesh.

For if ye live after the flesh, ye shall die: but if ye through the spirit do mortify the deeds of the body ye shall live.

For as many as are led by the Spirit of GOD, they are the sons of GOD.

The spiritual life is a new concept to you and amazing things can be seen as well as experienced. Give it time and be thankful, The Lord

is still molding us and guiding us.

You might want to think that the spiritual life and walking with the Lord are boring and you'll never measure up and meet his standards, that is just one of our many character defects in our thinking. Once you have a taste of the Lord's goodness, you won't want to ever go back to the way we once were. The character defects as I understand them could be chalked up to the seven deadly sins. Are we slower to anger? Are we less greedy? Are we not as lazy? Have we began developing new habits and making new friends? There will always be a few underlying defects that crop up and bother us. One of mine is commitment in the Lord's ministries. I find that I feel that I fall way short. This book is one of the primary parts of the ministry. In other areas, my friends from the bible study and all of their appointments to speak, I have missed out on. My friend Frank… I haven't been able to hook up with him, and I know he has a need. I've started into an area of work that is very demanding and I have struggled in that area and doing my best to cater to my wife and kids and the church. This new set of frustrations though we have to be patient through. My pastor announced today that he would be opening up Wednesday nights, once a month for those that would like an opportunity to preach and speak and share the word. This is something I've always wanted to do, but never felt worthy enough to do it. It scares me to death. But I am going to go through with it and pray about it and see if my pastor would run a van up to the VA and bring down my friends for the service. There is no pass or fail on this trial. There is only obedience to GOD'S word that is done out of Love for the glory of the Lord. That far outweighs any feelings and misgivings that I may have as I have described about being scared. Do you think that the disciples and apostles didn't get nervous? I will bet they did, for they had a learning curve in there while JESUS was teaching them. So this is how character defects get dealt with. Being patient, be willing, be watchful, The Lord provides the opportunities and doors are opening all around us even in a small place like Beaver Dams, New York. If I didn't have this chance in this part of my life now, I would still be carrying on my old behaviors of addiction and drinking and just might be in jail or dead. When I went to the Pastor's school conference, I stood up and made a commitment to help spread the gospel for my church that I attend and for future church planting and now that is being made a reality through our Lord and Saviour JESUS CHRIST only two months later when I was drawing my own conclusions which were not in line with the LORD'S. We are all not perfect at this, but we strive for progress... This is a lifelong endeavor which doesn't have to be boring. So if anyone says they are done with the steps and they have completed them, they are not telling the truth and have stopped their growth. For the reward of this process is as I described and more. The more is found in;

Romans 8: 15-18

For ye have not received the spirit of bondage again to fear; but ye have received the spirit of adoption, whereby we cry, ABBA, Father.

The spirit itself beareth witness with our spirit, that we are the children of GOD:

And if children, then heirs; heirs of GOD, and joint – heirs with CHRIST; if so be that we suffer with him, that we may be also glorified together.

For I reckon that the sufferings of this present time are not worthy to be compared with the glory which shall be revealed in us.

So my friends, be patient and continue on in seeking the Father's will for our lives. You will be in awe of the blessings that will be bestowed upon us as we walk this path. Even though we may think were ready to have our character defects removed...It is GOD who does it in his time according to his purpose for the greater good. God Bless.

Chapter 11

Step 7

Humbly asked him to remove our shortcomings and to stay focused on his will for our life.

This for me is a daily maintenance step to keep myself in check. It is designed for me to go to the Lord in prayer concerning my everyday behavior. When I'm cut off in traffic, How should I react? Hopefully, I will have forgiveness and a short prayer and not waving a fist or a finger. How should I be treating people in everyday life? I would hope for Loving kindness if you are to walk with the spirit of the Lord. Because rudeness, arrogance, acting puffed up will quench the spirit. Cursing is another way to quench the spirit. If you would, go back and read chapter 3 and the scripture of 1 Corinthians 13 concerning the example of how we are to live our life and for our life to work as we let go and let GOD do the leading. We still have to make an effort to temper our actions and responses.

We do this by being aware of the spirit that dwells within us. We make the effort to live by JESUS' examples. I find that when I am getting angry or frustrated, I need to go to the Lord in prayer because I'm trying to do things by my will and what I think is best. My will has never worked. I've always ended up stressed out and resentful, beaten, down on myself and joined to chaos. This step helps us to work on catching ourselves before we do some hideous action that will cause us to have to make an amends or suffer a consequence. WE will realize if we are at this point in our growth and walk with the Lord, that we have come much too far and done too much work to throw it away when we have such a great power through Christ who strengthens us. In our Bible;

Romans 8:35-39

Who shall separate us from the Love of CHRIST? Shall

tribulation, or distress, or persecution, or famine, or nakedness, or peril, or sword?

As it is written, for thy sake we are killed all the day long; we are accounted as sheep for the slaughter.

Nay, in all these things we are more than conquerors through him that loved us.

For I am persuaded that neither death, nor life, nor angels, nor principalities,

*nor powers, nor things
present, nor things to come,*

*Nor height, nor depth, nor
any other creature, shall be
able to separate us from
the Love of GOD which is
in CHRIST JESUS our
Lord.*

**About the only one who
can separate us from GOD
is our self. Romans 12
gives us another example
of how we are to live our
life in our walk with the
Lord.**

Romans 12: 1-21

I beseech you therefore, brethren, by the mercies of GOD, that ye present your bodies a living sacrifice, holy, acceptable unto GOD, which is your reasonable service.

And be not conformed to this world: but be ye transformed by the renewing of your mind,

*that ye may prove what is
that good, and acceptable,
and perfect, will of GOD.*

*For I say through the grace
given unto me, to every
man that is among you,
not to think of himself
more highly than he ought
to think; But to think
soberly, according as GOD
hath dealt to every man the
measure of faith.*

*For as we have many
members in one body, and*

all members have not the same office:

So we being many, are one body in CHRIST, and every one members of one another.

Having then gifts differing according to the grace that is given to us, whether prophecy, let us prophesy according to the proportion of faith;

Or ministry, Let us wait on our ministering: or he that teacheth, on teaching;

Or he that exhorteth, on exhortation: he that giveth, let him do it with simplicity; he that ruleth, with diligence; he that sheweth mercy, with cheerfulness.

Let love be without dissimulation. Abhor that which is evil; cleave to that which is good.

Be kindly affectioned one to another with brotherly love; in honour preferring one another ;

*Not slothful in business;
fervent in spirit; serving
the Lord.*

*Rejoicing in hope; patient
in tribulation; continuing
instant in prayer;*

*Distributing to the
necessity of saints; given to
hospitality.*

*Bless them which persecute
you: Bless and curse not.*

*Rejoice with them that do
rejoice, and weep with
them that weep.*

Be of the same mind one toward another. Mind not high things, but condescend to men of low estate. Be not wise in your own conceits.

Recompense to no man evil for evil. Provide things honest in the sight of all men.

If it be possible, as much lieth in you, live peaceably with all men.

Dearly beloved, avenge not yourselves, but rather give

place unto wrath: for it is written, vengeance is mine; I will repay saith the Lord.

Therefore if thine enemy hunger, feed him; if he thirst, give him drink: for in so doing thou shalt heap coals of fire on his head.

Be not overcome with evil, but overcome evil with good.

Once we can start realizing our shortcomings, which are those lusts that war

against our souls that lead us to old behaviors and our old ways, we can with CHRIST'S blessing overcome them and turn them around. If you used to deal drugs, you might be a good in business negotiations or as a purchasing agent. We already know how to network and find the best deals. Look at our talents and experience that we have and use them for good. Could you tell your story to young people at schools or churches to help deter them from the experiences that we went through? I'm writing this book to help share my experience. I'm working on pamphlets to assist people with a start in recovery to a new life. My life previous to this was hanging out with people full of empty promises...drinking and using. My life is being changed, and I have become more aware of what's healthy and what's not. I am being restored and strengthened; I owe the glory to the Lord.

Romans 13:8-14

Owe no man anything, but to love one another: for he that loveth another hath fulfilled the law.

For this, Thou shalt not commit adultery, Thou shalt not kill, Thou shalt not steal, Thou shalt not bear false witness, Thou shalt not covet; and if there be any other commandment, it is briefly comprehended in this saying, namely, Thou shalt love thy neighbor as thyself.

Love worketh no ill to his neighbor: therefore love is the fulfilling of the law.

The night is far spent, the day is at hand: let us therefore cast off the works of darkness, and let us put on the armor of light.

Let us walk honestly, as in the day, not in rioting and drunkenness, not in chambering and wantonness, not in strife and envying

But put ye on the Lord JESUS CHRIST, and make not provision for the flesh, to fulfill the lusts thereof.

Chapter 12

Step 8

Made a list of all the people we had harmed and became willing to make amends to them all.

This is actually a very simple step involving making a list and becoming willing. Let's just hope the writer's cramp don't kill us or discourage us from the length of the list. I'm chuckling as I write that last statement. My list was pretty long, and I'm still working through it. There isn't a time limit on this, but be willing, because you never know when you may run across someone you have hurt or you may encounter someone you forgot about that is still harboring ill feelings. Let us make amends with our Lord and Savior first and foremost, because without him you have absolutely nothing! Let us not forget about ourselves and the amends we make. Our amends to ourselves is living a new life according to God's word. We also need to be looking at the harm we've done to our families, wives, husbands, significant others, Moms and dads, brothers and sisters, our kids and so the list goes on. Some amends may go well and the party that has been wronged might be understanding, but if they are not then you pray about it and don't cause more harm and don't go drinking and using over it if your amends wasn't welcome. Remember actions speak louder than words, people will see the true change and sometimes it takes time. Every time we need to put it in the Lord's hands.

Go look in the mirror and ask for forgiveness and make a commitment to yourself to lead your new life. If you can look yourself in the mirror and make that commitment, then you are ready to take this step to the next level. Talk with your pastor and counselors about this and get some more insight. This is helpful to have so you don't make more of a mess. When we do this list, we are looking only at our actions, and we need to have that person in a neutral state so to speak, whether you like that person or not. Do not pre-judge people, for it will be healthier to you if you look at it in this sense. We don't look at the wrongs they have done to us. This is about what we did. Remember, we are setting things right for the Lord and for us. Look at the story of Saul before he was transformed and became Paul. Saul hurt a lot of the disciples and persecuted them. The Lord

Blinded him for three days, he was dropped to the ground and receiving pin pricks to the heart for the persecutions of the Saints in Jerusalem. He had a serious amends to make to the Lord. That story is in the book of *Acts chapter 9.* I encourage you to look it up and read it, his list was pretty involved too. So GOD didn't kill him, that is how merciful GOD is, how forgiving and how much grace he has. GOD won't kill you either... so let's be willing. Trust, Faith, and Belief are the key elements here. Don't let the tapes run through your head, don't play out scenarios in your mind, just make the list with no reservation.

Chapter 13

Step 9

Made direct amends to such people wherever possible except when to do so would injure them or others and yourself.

You will need wisdom, knowledge, courage, faith, and a sincere desire. A lot of prayer too. If you are viewing things in a different manner, then you are probably ready to

take this step. Walk humbly, for it is time to let the new inner man or woman shine through. I understand just how my previous life with my wife and children was so screwed up. To understand that, that was a gift from GOD. A real eye opener. I was the one with the wrong perception. The wrongs I believed that had been done to me were not relevant. GOD took those from me and restored me. I no longer hated my wife, I wasn't bitter anymore towards my step son or my family. In doing this amends step, I was very humbled. GOD had me sharing a wisdom and love with my wife from the new inner man unlike anything I had ever experienced before in my life. I was able to talk and communicate just what I had done wrong and what I needed to do to change.

My wife listened with surprise and listened very intently. I shared my fears with her rather than the macho egotistical man who thinks he has a plan. I told her from the heart how I failed to love her correctly according to GOD'S standards. It was sincerity and the love of GOD that has set us on a new path. Being reunited with my wife and children has been a blessing. A true reward for putting the effort into the getting to know the Lord and working the steps from a biblical standpoint. The saying "Love Wins" rings true. Some amends may not go this well, it takes two willing people who want resolution. Some may have a lot of bitterness and you may have to endure a chewing out, but don't say anything derogatory in return that may cause more hurt. Let your inner person shine through, some amends may take time and all you can do is pray about it and let your actions shine through. The amends process is a lifelong endeavor. It's about doing what is right and if we choose to do it only partway right, we will hurt ourselves and cause greater harm to the parties that we have injured already. So I don't mean to say that it will never come to an end. I mean to say we have to walk with the mindset and a pure heart before the Lord daily and how we conduct our self will reveal our true motives and intent. Some amends may be done through letters and explanations over a period of time. If you have thefts and robberies to deal with, maybe an anonymous letter and repayment for their loss would be appropriate. Use discretion, but do not ignore this. Payments and explanations could be done through a pastor who is supportive of your recovery. This way you are not harming yourself and you may be giving some closure to the parties affected. In doing so, you are undoing the evil ways of Satan and working towards the Lords goal for you. You will be discovering a greater freedom and peace. This brings us to Wisdom; Remember in Proverbs?

Wisdom is the principle thing.

Her ways are ways of pleasantness, and all her paths are peace.

Forsake her not!

For she is thy life.

So don't mess with wisdom and try to pull a folly on her. She and the Lord will nail your keister to the wall come judgment time. Walk humbly and do your best, with this step. We learned how to get drunk and strung out on drugs when we were at our best in our sinful ways. Well now we have to do our best with these steps and for the Lord. We won't be perfect because we are still on this earth and in our fleshy bodies. We won't be made perfect until JESUS comes and calls us home. Give yourself a chance to experience the reward,

you owe it to yourself.
That feeling of love, joy,
and happiness and peace.
Best cure there is.

Chapter 14

Step 10

Continued to take personal inventory and when we were wrong, promptly admitted it through prayer.

I hope I never forget this process of taking inventory due to the reward of wisdom and peace that comes along. I found myself being very selfish one night... I came home expected my

children to be fed and put to bed. Boy did I get angry! I yelled at my kids and accused my wife of ignoring those responsibilities. Little did I know at that time that I was to blame. My wife had already told me of her workload between working and going to school. She did tell me she wouldn't have a lot of time for the kids and her normal duties. The next morning I got a glimpse of her pain that she felt through all of the stress and anguish, The Lord opened my eyes to it that morning and as I listened to her, I felt the tears well up in my eyes because I just realized how selfish I was to act like an idiot that previous night. I was fully utterly and completely wrong and convicted of the truth. I told her just that. I apologized and she thanked me and told me it takes a true man to admit and say what I had said. She went to work or school that morning, can't remember which, but she had a smile on her face along with peace. That was and is a true blessing from our Lord and Saviour JESUS CHRIST. I had a rush of peace come over me knowing I had done the will of GOD and that it was pleasing to GOD to see me do that and follow through. The Wisdom is so beautiful, words can't describe. Exhilarating and breathless is as close as I could come to describing it with great gratitude. So keep watch and humble yourself to the Lord and he will show you a great many things. It is never a boring journey.

Chapter 15

Step 11

Sought through prayer and meditation to improve our conscious contact with GOD and Jesus as we understand him, praying only for the knowledge of his will for us and the power to carry that out.

I know when God speaks through the spirit, he answers my prayers and we have to know how to

pray. We don't ask for material possessions or money. We ask for guidance, faith, grace, mercy, wisdom, strength, peace, Love, humbleness, forgiveness, obedience, patience. Our task in this step is to learn how to pray and sit quietly focusing in on GOD and his Son, Lord JESUS CHRIST. Another one who you wish to learn about is the Holy Spirit and his function. GOD'S will for me is a very good study topic and I couldn't have written this book without doing my homework and listening to the Lord. Another good topic for finding out what the will of the Father is for our life is "The fear of the Lord" and understanding what kind of blessing this truly is. This is an absolute necessity as a pre-requisite. After all, if we are to follow the Lord's will for our lives, don't we need to know who we are following even better? In order to gain a true understanding? You see if our focus is on the Lord's will, then we won't have time for an addiction. We will have been delivered from those bonds of fear…No more captivity unless you make the choice and resort back to ignorance and choose to suffer the consequences seven-fold and I doubt you would live through it.

If you have come this far, take a look at how far you've come and reflect for a moment, then start looking forward again. Make a gratitude list and thank the Lord for all the wonderful blessings. Don't let it go...Get involved in the Lord's work, go and join a mission field. Let everyone know what the Lord has done for you. This step does involve a complete surrender of our

will each and every day.
You see, we live in
perilous or evil times and
our Lord JESUS CHRIST
and GOD the Father has
only three or four
requirements for us in
these end times.

Preach the gospel of
JESUS CHRIST to all the
world.

Everything you do, you do
out of love unto the Lord.

Keep their Commandments in your heart and live by them.

Help feed the fatherless and the widows.

In that last one, it isn't just food that we eat every day, its more than that. It is the word of God that we need to feed them. Fatherless means without JESUS CHRIST, because unless you acknowledge the Son of God, you have nothing but a ticket to hell. You may think you are the most caring and giving person around, but if you have not the love of JESUS, you have nothing. Go read it for yourself in 1 Corinthians 13. JESUS CHRIST died for all the people in the world. He took all our sin upon him and laid down his life out of LOVE so that we may have an easier way to salvation through faith, belief and repentance.

Romans 10:9

If thou shalt confess with thy mouth the Lord JESUS, and shalt believe in thine heart that GOD hath raised him from the dead, thou shalt be saved.

So if this is not true, then where are the sacrificial altars?

Where are your oxen, bullocks, goats and sheep for your sin sacrifice?

That is why in the earlier part of the book, I explained the two covenants. JESUS was tempted by Satan and offered all the nations of the world if he would only bow down to Satan. The big deception here is that only the nations were offered and people were not included. People claim the bible is too hard to understand, that's just a lame excuse for procrastination. We go to college to learn the warped ways of the world and man which is a lot more confusing than what the word of GOD is by far. Shame on our ignorance! It is not yet too late to learn about who GOD is. It takes knowledge, dedication and understanding to gain the wisdom we need to be free from the bonds of man and the world. I wrote the 11th step in this fashion because for me it is a daily step of a lifelong process. I also did it this way to show you a different sort of life, that when you embrace it, it was what you were seeking all along. But our decisions to turn to the drugs and the alcohol and sexual addictions have kept the Spirit of GOD away from you. May GOD bless you and keep you, may His light shine upon you. In JESUS CHRIST'S Name, Amen.

Chapter 16

Step 12

Having had a Spiritual Awakening as the result of these steps, we tried to carry this message to alcoholics & addicts and people of all walks of life, and to practice these principles in all our affairs.

Let this awakening shine through. The Glory belongs to the Lord and it is your duty to tell about

it. My friend Mike Crook shared with me a couple of verses and I would like to share them with you.

Isaiah 60:1

Arise, Shine; For thy light is come and the Glory of the Lord is risen upon thee.

Isaiah 61:1,2,3

The Spirit of the Lord GOD is upon me; because the Lord hath anointed me to preach good tidings unto the meek; he hath sent me to bind up the brokenhearted, to proclaim liberty to the captives, and the opening of the prison to them that are bound;

To proclaim the acceptable year of the Lord, and the day of vengeance of our GOD to comfort all that mourn;

To appoint unto them that mourn in ZION, to give unto them Beauty for ashes, the oil of Joy for mourning, the garment of praise for the spirit of *heaviness; that they might be called trees of righteousness, the planting of the Lord, that he might be glorified.*

In Isaiah 61:1, that is our instruction for how we should live our life. Helping those who are lost find the Lord. For are we not mourning because of the mess we have created in the life we were given?

Have we not burned our life to ashes? Do we not carry the spirit of heaviness?

Does not JESUS CHRIST offer us a fresh start to a new life?

There is a great joy and peace in following the Lord's will for our lives. The rewards are far greater than what our imaginations can dream up or comprehend. When you may have a bad day in the world, you can still have peace and smile. That's how powerful the Lord's blessing are.

In Isaiah 60:1 This verse touches us in ways that are so wonderful, that it greatly outweighs any desire we may think we have.

In the Spiritual Awakening, God truly sets us free. I have to disagree with some of the 12 step groups that claim we only have a daily reprieve and that we are not cured. As long as we walk in the light of the Lord, he is the cure. It for me is like calling GOD weak, and doubting that he has the power to heal us. Woe to them that speak in this manner. Did not Jesus heal the lepers, make the blind to see, heal the deaf, cast out demons, and allow the lame to walk? Those weren't just temporary fixes. They were permanent. Are we not blind and lame as well if we don't accept CHRIST into our heart? These 12 steps are a guideline for us to follow as we are re-directed from our destructive path to grow and mature. To gain knowledge and understanding in order to find wisdom in sight of our Heavenly Father while we still have time.

It has been indeed a pleasure to write this book

for the glory of our Lord. This task was given to me by the Lord and he decides what goes in, where it starts and where it ends.

Psalms 34:1-22

I will bless the Lord at all times: His praise shall be continually in my mouth.

My soul shall make her boast in the Lord: the humble shall hear thereof, and be glad.

O magnify the Lord with me, and let us exalt his name together.

I sought the Lord, and he heard me, and delivered me from all my fears.

They looked unto him, and were lightened: and their faces were not ashamed.

This poor man cried, and the Lord heard him, and saved him out of all his troubles.

The angel of the Lord encampeth round about

them that fear him, and deliEDITreth them.

O taste and see that the Lord is good: Blessed is the man that trusteth in him.

O fear the Lord, ye his saints: for there is no want to them that fear him.

The young lions do lack, and suffer hunger: but they that seek the Lord shall not want any good thing.

Come, ye children, hearken unto me: I will teach you the fear of the Lord.

What man is he that desireth life and loveth many days, that he may see good?

Keep thy tongue from evil, and thy lips from speaking guile.

Depart from evil, and do good; seek peace and pursue it.

The eyes of the Lord are upon the righteous, and his ears are open unto their cry.

The face of the Lord is against them that do evil, to cut off the remembrance of them from the earth.

The righteous cry, and the Lord heareth, and delivereth them out of all their troubles.

The Lord is nigh unto them that are of a broken heart; and saveth such as be of a contrite spirit.

Many are the afflictions of the righteous: but the Lord delivereth him out of all.

He keepeth all his bones: not one of them is broken.

Evil shall slay the wicked: and they that hate the righteous shall be desolate.

The Lord redeemeth the soul of his servants: and none of them that trust in him shall be desolate.

This is a Psalms that helped to change my life, when I was in the VA, my spirit was broken. I was living in fear of the world and what the countries

and their governments were doing. I felt as though there was no hope. This Psalm was a calling of my soul and my being to be reconciled with GOD. It was then that I knew GOD was wanting me and he had a purpose for me. I felt renewed hope and a desire to know who GOD and JESUS CHRIST truly are. I had the determination of the shepherd boy David to know GOD'S heart. My focus was shifted from my pathetic outlook to diving into finding out who GOD really is, what he requires of us and how he conducts himself and why. This journey began a year ago, and it has been a wonderful journey of knowledge and enlightenment, and instruction and wisdom. This has been a blessing in my life so fascinating, seeing my life re-shaped and re-directed and totally rebuilt by the LORD. A special thanks goes to the staff members of the VA in Bath, New York for their support and instruction and guidance in my time of need and cry for help.

Thank you.

In Closing...

I study every day and there is always something new to experience. I pray many times each day, thanking GOD for the blessings he has given to my life. I do not regret my past. I have no desire to pick up a drink or a drug today. God has delivered me from that captivity. I know that if I choose to go back to my old ways of life, the penalty will be severe and of an unknown consequence seven-fold. Staying on this path and seeing GOD at work in my life is a whole lot better than what the world has to offer.

The prayer of intercession;

These words spake JESUS, and lifted his eyes to heaven, and said, Father, the hour is come: Glorify thy Son, that thy Son also may Glorify thee:

As thou hast given him power over all flesh, that he should give eternal life to as many as thou hast given him.

And this is life eternal, that they might know thee the only true GOD, and JESUS CHRIST, whom thou hast sent.

I have glorified thee on the earth: I have finished the

*work which thou gavest
me to do.*

*And now, O Father,
Glorify thou me with thine
own self with the glory
which I had with thee
before the world was.*

*I have manifested thy
name unto the men which
thou gavest me out of the
world: Thine they were and
thou gavest them me; and
they have kept thy word.*

Now they have known that all things whatsoever thou hast given me are of thee.

For I have given unto them the words which thou gavest me; and they have received them, and have known surely that I came out from thee, and they have believed that thou didst send me.

I pray for them: I pray not for the world, but for them which thou hast given me; for they are thine.

And all mine are thine, and thine are mine; and I am glorified in them.

And now I am no more in the world, but these are in the world, and I come to thee. Holy Father, keep through thine own name those whom thou hast given me, that they may be one, as we are.

While I was with them in the world, I kept them in thy name: Those that thou gavest me I have kept, and *none of them is lost, But the son of perdition; that the scripture might be fulfilled.*

And now I come to thee; and these things I speak in the world, that they might have my joy fulfilled in themselves.

I have given them thy word; and the world hath hated them, because they are not of the world, even as I am not of the world.

I pray not that thou shouldest take them out of the world, but that thou shouldest keep them from evil.

They are not of the world, even as I am not of the world,

Sanctify them through thy truth: thy word is truth.

As thou has sent me into the world, even so have I also sent them into the world.

And for their sakes I sanctify myself, that they also might be sanctified through the truth.

Neither pray I for these alone, but for them also which shall believe on me through their word;

That they may all be one; as thou, art in me, and I in thee, that they also may be one in us: that the world may believe that thou hast sent me.

And the glory which thou gavest me I have given them: that they may be one, even as we are one:

I in them, and thou in me, that they may be made perfect in one: and that the world may know that thou hast sent me, and hast loved them, as thou loved me.

Father, I will that they also, whom thou hast given me, be with me where I am: that they may behold my glory, which thou hast given me: for thou lovedst me before the foundation of the world.

O righteous Father, the world hath not known thee: and these have known that thou sent me.

And I have declared unto them thy name, and will declare it: that the love wherewith thou hast loved me may be in them and I in them.

The grace that was bestowed upon JESUS was and is a very beautiful gift. We too, can experience the gift of grace if we choose to live for the truth.

GOD Bless Brothers and Sisters

A Minister of GOD

Glossary

Abomination- **Anything that arouses strong disgust.**

Admonishing- **To advise about ones faults or warn against something in order that one may be guided to improve.**

Afflictions- **A state of pain, trouble, or distress; misery**

Blasphemy- **Abuse of or contempt for GOD or sacred things.**

Bowels-Figurative; pity, or tender feelings.

Chambering- A person who frequents the ladies.

Clamorous- Loud and noisy; shouting, making noisy demands or complaints.

Concupiscence- Desires or Lusts.

Condescend- To stoop or lower one's self.

Confounded- Confused; disordered, damned, hateful or detestable.

Consecrated- To set apart as sacred; make holy

Covenant- Solemn promises of GOD to man as set forth in the old and New testaments

Covet- To desire something that belongs to another.

Covetnous- Greedy

Dissimulation- Deceit, Hypocrisies

Doctrine- What is taught

Ensample- Example

Envieth- Wanting what one has; discontent

Exhort- To urge strongly; advise or warn strongly.

Exhorting- To give earnest advice or warning.

Forbearing- To hold back; keep from doing, saying or using.

Froward- Not easily managed.

Gentiles- Non Jewish

Guile- **Crafty deceit; cunning; crafty behavior; sly tricks.**

Hastened- **To cause to go faster. Quicken**

Hearken- **To pay close attention to what is said.**

Hewn- **To cut, shape or form. (past tense).**

Honoureth- **Integrity, uprightness, honesty, To hold in high regard.**

Idolatry- **The worship of idols. The paying or**

offering of divine honors to any created object.

Iniquities- A wicked or unjust acts.

Intercession- The act or fact of interceding; pleading for another.

Lucre- money considered as a bad or degrading influence.

Malice- An active ill will, A wish to hurt or cause harm or make to suffer.

Mediator- To be a go-between to settle

argument or reach agreement.

Meekness- Gentle, courteous, kind, merciful, compassionate.

Mingle- To bring together, unite, or join.

Mortify- To overcome bodily desires and feelings by going without things.

Peril- The chance of harm, loss, destruction or danger.

Principalities- JESUS' place and rank of Authority

Prudence- Wise thought before acting; Good judgment, Foresight.

Puffed Up- Conceited, Pretentious, EGO driven.

Redemption- Deliverance from sin through JESUS CHRIST (Romans 10:9)

Reproveth- Expressing disapproval without scolding and with the purpose of hope of correcting the fault.

Rebuke- To express disapproval of; scolding.

Remission- Pardon, Forgiveness of sins.

Sanctifieth- To make holy; To set apart as sacred.

Slothful- Unwilling, Lazy, Idle

Strife- The act of quarreling; fighting; contentious.

Suffereth- To have pain, grief, or injury.

Tabernacle- A place of worship.

Testament- Written instructions of what to do after one's death

Transgressions- A breaking of GOD'S Laws.

Unseemingly- Improper, Indecent.

Vaunteth- Boasting, Bragging, Proud, Vain

Vigilant- Observant, Watchful, Wide-awake, Cautious

Wantonness- Reckless, Heartless, or Malicious.

Zion- Heaven, as the final home of those who are virtuous and truly devout.

Notes

Notes

Notes

www.ingramcontent.com/pod-product-compliance
Lightning Source LLC
Chambersburg PA
CBHW062124280526
45788CB00001B/48